Bond

10 Minute Tests

11⁺-12⁺ years

Sarah Lindsay

Maths

Nelson Thornes

TEST 1: **Shape and Space**

1

Draw the net of a cube.

3-4

Plot the coordinates (3, 2), (−3, −2), (−1, 2) and (1, −2) on this grid.

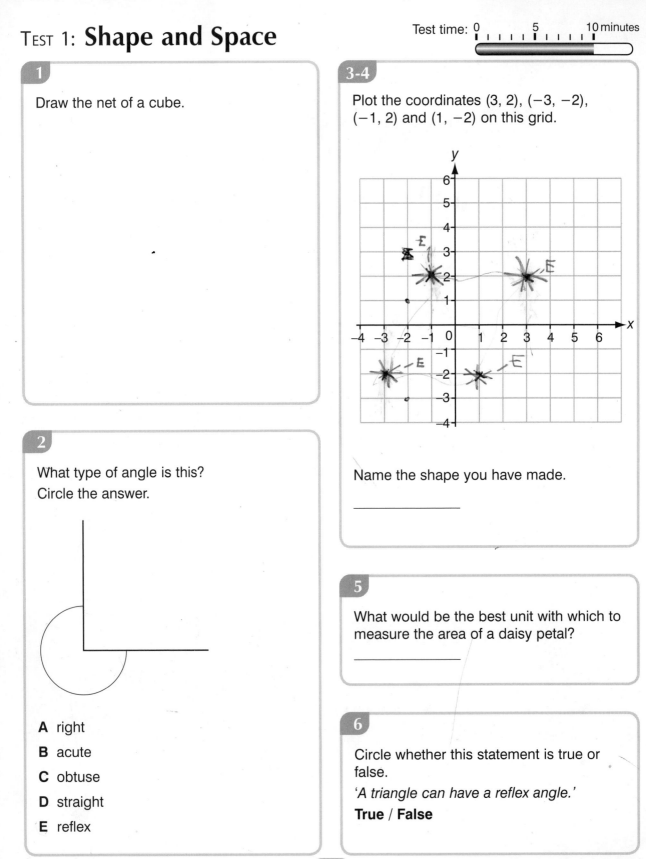

Name the shape you have made.

_____

2

What type of angle is this?
Circle the answer.

A right

B acute

C obtuse

D straight

E reflex

5

What would be the best unit with which to measure the area of a daisy petal?

_____

6

Circle whether this statement is true or false.
'*A triangle can have a reflex angle.*'
True / False

7

The area of a rectangle is 72 cm². Its long sides are double the length of its short sides. How long is a short side?

Circle the answer.

A 6 cm

B 7.2 cm

C 14 cm

D 18 cm

E 36 cm

8

Draw the reflection of this shape in the lines of symmetry.

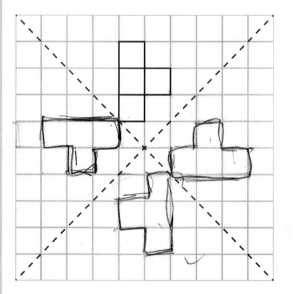

9

What are the missing angles?

134°

134°

x   x

$x =$ _____

10

Name this shape.

_____

Total

1

Approximately which number is the arrow pointing to?

Circle the answer.

0 _____↑_____ 1.5

A 5   **B** 1   **C** 0.75   **D** 0.5   **E** 0.07

2

$(45 \div 9) \times (100 \div 10) + (23 - 19) =$ ____

3

Place these fractions in order, largest first.

$$\frac{3}{7} \quad \frac{17}{15} \quad \frac{3}{4} \quad \frac{8}{9} \quad \frac{12}{6}$$

_____

4

What is the square root of 121?   ____

5

The time is 13:16.

Finn has 51 minutes until his maths test finishes. What will the time be then?

6

Complete this number sentence with the missing signs (< or >).

(23 + 56) ____ **(19 + 64)** ____ **74**

74

7

Lynn wants to buy a jacket. The jacket is £75 but is on sale for 15% off. How much will the jacket cost Lynn?

Circle the answer.

A £60.00

B £70.50

C £63.75

D £11.25

E £50.00

8

What is $8 \times \frac{5}{7}$?   ____

9

A car travelled at 80 mph for 20 miles before being stopped by the police. How long did it take the car to travel this distance?

____ minutes

10

Round 26.785 litres to the nearest tenth of a litre.

____ litres

Total ____

TEST 3: Algebra

1

What is y if $56y = 728$?

Circle the answer.

A 13

B 12

C 11

D 10

E 9

2

Write this algebraic expression in its simplest form.

$t + t + t + t - r$

_____

3-4

Which of the following functions, when added to this function machine, will give the largest and smallest outputs?

Write the correct letters on the answer lines below.

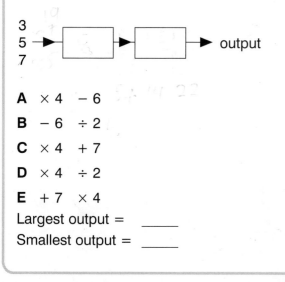

3
5 → [ ] → [ ] → output
7

A × 4 − 6

B − 6 ÷ 2

C × 4 + 7

D × 4 ÷ 2

E + 7 × 4

Largest output = _____

Smallest output = _____

5

Continue this sequence.

−29 **−16** **−3** ____ ____ ____

6

Use algebra to simplify this sentence.

3 more than k plus 8 less than m

_____

7

Alice thinks of a number, she doubles it and then adds 19. The answer is 89. What is the number she was thinking of?

Circle the answer.

A 70

B 26

C 62

D 35

E 45

8

Solve this equation if $x = 15$ and $y = -3$.

$3x + y =$ _____

9

Find the value of a.

$5a + 4 = 49$ $a =$ _____

10

Complete the missing number in the equation.

If $27 \div r = 2 + 1$ then $r \times \square = 27$

5

Total

Test time: 0 ··········· 5 ··········· 10 minutes

1-2

These pie charts show the animals that visited Blackmore Vets Surgery over two consecutive weeks.

Week 1 (80 animals)

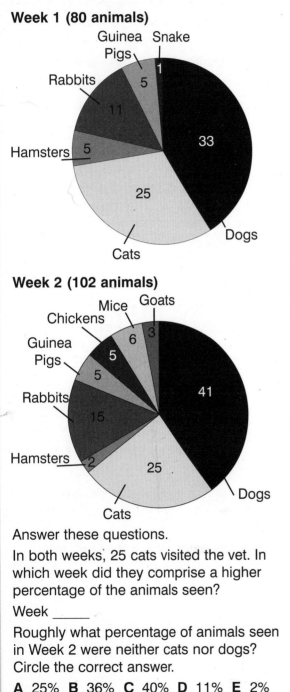

Week 2 (102 animals)

Answer these questions.

In both weeks, 25 cats visited the vet. In which week did they comprise a higher percentage of the animals seen?

Week _____

Roughly what percentage of animals seen in Week 2 were neither cats nor dogs? Circle the correct answer.

A 25% **B** 36% **C** 40% **D** 11% **E** 2%

3 ✳

A teacher decides to give her class an algebra assessment. When she collates the results she wants to see if there is any pattern between the ability of both boys and girls and the months in which they were born. What information will the teacher need in order to carry out this task?

a _____

_____

_____

_____

_____

b _____

_____

_____

_____

_____

c _____

_____

_____

_____

_____

Daniel keeps chickens and sells the eggs that are laid. He keeps a record of the number of eggs that are laid each day for two weeks. Illustrate this data as accurately as possible in a bar chart.

Mon	Tue	Wed	Thu	Fri	Sat	Sun
27	24	25	23	20	28	25
Mon	Tue	Wed	Thu	Fri	Sat	Sun
23	21	27	25	24	21	28

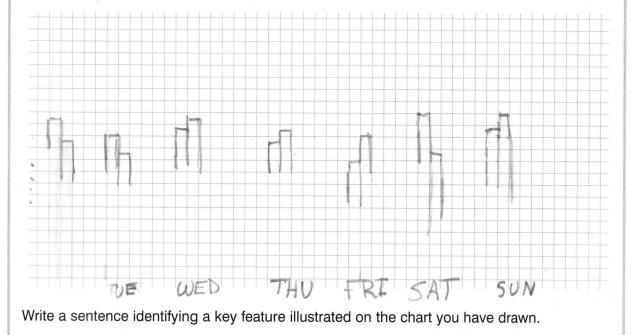

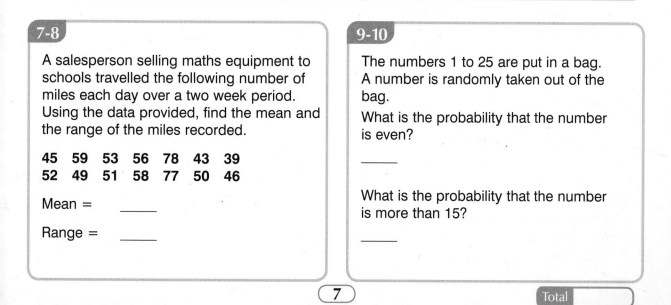

Write a sentence identifying a key feature illustrated on the chart you have drawn.

_____

_____

_____

A salesperson selling maths equipment to schools travelled the following number of miles each day over a two week period. Using the data provided, find the mean and the range of the miles recorded.

45 59 53 56 78 43 39
52 49 51 58 77 50 46

Mean = _____

Range = _____

The numbers 1 to 25 are put in a bag. A number is randomly taken out of the bag.

What is the probability that the number is even?

_____

What is the probability that the number is more than 15?

_____

Total

TEST 5: **Number**

1

Write a number sentence that will equal the target number 67.8.

_____

2

Double $4\frac{3}{5}$ _____

3

If 50 tubes of sweets cost £24.00, how much would one tube cost?

Circle the answer.

A 24p **B** 5p   **C** 48p **D** 50p **E** 2p

4

Write the number one hundred and four thousand point six.

_____

5

Circle the number that equals 27×6.

161   **126**   **162**   **116**   **164**   **146**

6

Complete this number pattern.

_____ _____ _____ **−1** _____ **5** _____

7

Add <, > or = so that the following makes sense.

$\frac{2}{3}$ _____ **0.7**

8

Ruth's grandmother decided to give each of her 11 grandchildren £35.00.
How much money did she give in total?
Circle the answer.

A £350

B £355

C £361

D £365

E £385

9

In a year group of 95 children, there is a ratio of brown eyes to blue eyes of 35 : 60. What is this ratio written in its simplest form?

Circle the answer.

A 8 : 15

B 7 : 12

C 18 : 30

D 14 : 24

E 7 : 21

10

How many more is 56 900.2 than 56 650.2?
Circle the answer.

A 20

B 200

C 250

D 300

E 350

Total

TEST 6: **Data Handling**

1

Write the probability that a coin will fall on heads. _____

2-4

This data shows the number of pets each family in a class owns.

Find the mean, median and mode of this data.

0	1	1	2	1	1	0	4	2	2	3	2
3	2	1	3	2	1	1	2	1	2	2	4
2	4	6	2	1	0	3	2	2	2	0	0

Mean = _____   Median = _____

Mode = _____

5-6

Look at this line graph.

Average House Price in Swellstown

What does this line graph show?

_____

_____

Why is the information shown in this line graph misleading?

_____

_____

7-8

You have been asked to carry out a survey on the amount of glass recycled by each household in a street near you.

List two questions you would include in your survey.

a _____

_____

_____

_____

b _____

_____

_____

_____

What would be the best way to display your results?

_____

9

Write this proportion as a fraction in its lowest terms.

12 out of 36 _____

10

This data shows the number of packets of sweets sold each hour at a music festival. Find the range of this data.

12 14 18 9 21 14 15 11 12 15

Range = _____

Time for a break! Go to Puzzle Page 42 ▶

Total _____

1

Write a definition for the word *congruent*.

_____

_____

_____

2

Describe the translation this shape has made.

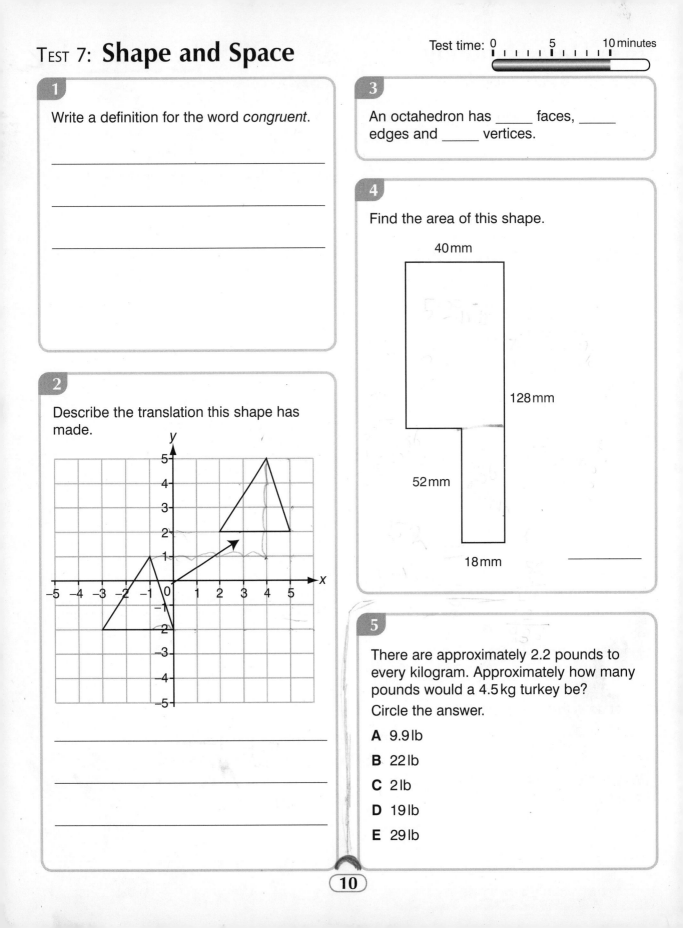

_____

_____

_____

3

An octahedron has _____ faces, _____ edges and _____ vertices.

4

Find the area of this shape.

40mm

128mm

52mm

18mm

_____

5

There are approximately 2.2 pounds to every kilogram. Approximately how many pounds would a 4.5kg turkey be?

Circle the answer.

A 9.9lb

B 22lb

C 2lb

D 19lb

E 29lb

What are the two missing angles?

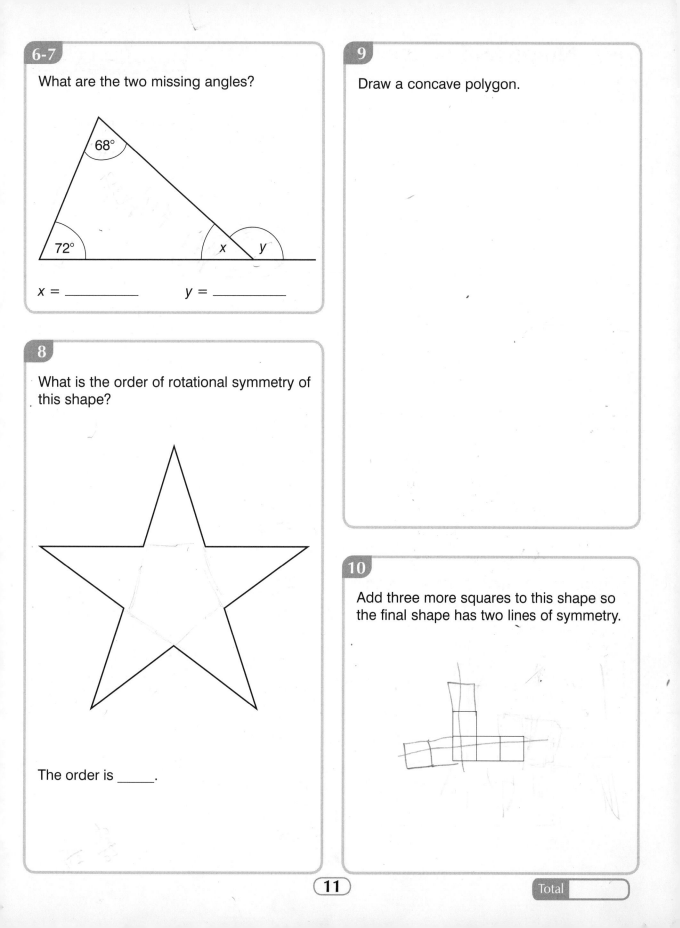

x = _____   y = _____

9

Draw a concave polygon.

8

What is the order of rotational symmetry of this shape?

The order is _____.

10

Add three more squares to this shape so the final shape has two lines of symmetry.

1

List all the factors of 32.

_____

_____

2

Round 4598.23 to the nearest 10.

_____

3

$-56.7 + 23.2 =$ _____

23.2   56.7
        272

4

70 litres of juice were prepared for a 24 hour football match. At the end of the match 15% of the total amount was left.

How much juice was left? _____ litres

5

In which set of numbers are all the numbers exactly divisible by 7?
Circle the answer.

A 164, 120, 108

B 156, 132, 96

C 138, 127, 81

D 161, 112, 91

E 153, 129, 95

6

Order these fractions from the smallest to the largest.

$\frac{5}{10}$ $\frac{3}{5}$ $\frac{9}{11}$ $\frac{73}{100}$ $\frac{1}{4}$

_____   _____   _____   _____   _____

7

Jay's dad had to go away on business. He left on Thursday 24th January at 6.30 a.m. and returned 11 days 14 hours later. What day, date and time did he return?

_____

8

Find the answer to 4.9×8 _____

9

Convert 500 000 cm into km.
Circle the answer.

A 0.005 km

B 0.05 km

C 5 km

D 50 km

E 500 km

10

$100^2 =$ _____

12

Total

TEST 9: Shape and Space

1

Three vertices of a kite are plotted in the first quadrant at (5, 3), (3, 6) and (5, 7). What are the coordinates of the fourth vertex?

(_____ , _____)

2

If the perimeter of a rectangle is 26 cm and its area is 40 cm², what are the lengths of its long and short sides?

Circle the answer.

A 6 cm and 7 cm

B 4 cm and 10 cm

C 2 cm and 20 cm

D 5 cm and 8 cm

E 13 cm and 2 cm

3-4

Draw the net of a triangular prism.

How many vertices does this 3-D shape have? _____

5-6

How many lines of symmetry does this parallelogram have? _____

State its order of rotational symmetry.

_____

7

Write something you would measure in kilometres.

_____

8

Calculate the missing angle in this triangle.

$x = $ _____

9

Write the name of the 3-D shape a football represents.

_____

10

If 1 inch equals 2.5 cm, how many inches are there in 1.5 metres?

_____ inches

13

Total

TEST 10: **Number**

1

Find the total length.

98 cm + 2.67 m − 67 mm = _____ cm

2

Add together all the prime numbers between 10 and 20. _____

3

Tom was given £90.00 for his birthday. He spent £29.99 on a new computer game, £45.49 on new trainers and put £10.00 in his savings account. How much money did he have left?

_____

4

$3 \times \frac{2}{5}$ = _____

5

Circle the smallest number.

A 0.35   **B** 0.129

C 0.471   **D** 0.5

E 0.511

6

Use all three numbers to make a number sentence that totals −7.

_____

7

The Painter family had to travel a total of 156.8 miles to get home. They stopped after 97.7 miles for a break. How much further did they have to travel?

_____ miles

8

Add the missing sign (< or >).

72% ☐ $\frac{14}{20}$

9

What is the lowest common multiple of 7 and 9?

Circle the answer.

A 3

B 16

C 49

D 56

E 63

10

Circle the best approximation of 23 989 ÷ 199.

A 120

B 122

C 119

D 124

E 125

Total ☐

TEST 11: **Algebra**

1

Which of the following algebraic expressions are written in their simplest form? Circle the answer.

i $a \times 4$ **ii** $b^2 - 7$

iii $2n + n$ **iv** $5t - t + 2$

v $6d - 2d$ **vi** $4 + y$

A *i, ii, iii*   **B** *iii, iv, vi*

C *ii, vi*   **D** *iii, v*

E *ii, iv*

2

If each term is 3 less than the seven times table what will the first four terms of the sequence be?

_____   _____   _____   _____

3

Look carefully at the grid below. Write the equation that represents the coordinates plotted. It may help to write out the coordinate pairs.

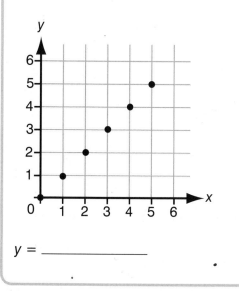

$y =$ _____

4-5

If the row values total 26 and the column values also total 26, what are the values of the letters *a* and *b*?

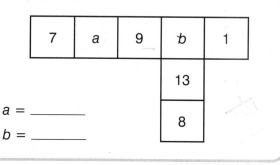

$a =$ _____

$b =$ _____

6

What is the fifth square number?

_____

7

Find the correct input for this function machine.

_____ → −5 → ×2 → 22

8

Find the total if $x = 6$ and $y = 2$.

$(6x \div 2) + 3y =$ _____

9-10

Write an equation for the following puzzle, then solve it.

Multiply *f* by 5, then add 16 to get a total of 61.

_____

$f =$ _____

Total

1-3

In order to decide on weight restrictions on their roads, Wiltshire Borough Council carry out an annual survey on the number of lorries that use some of their lanes. They have surveyed the same roads for the past 5 years. The following table shows the results.

Lane	Average number of lorries per weekday				
	Year 1	Year 2	Year 3	Year 4	Year 5
Tetbury Lane	12	34	32	26	44
Charlton Lane	18	27	25	18	29
Hankerton Lane	32	34	36	41	56
Oaksey Lane	10	14	14	15	16
Milbourne Lane	32	39	41	50	48

Which lane has seen the biggest increase in lorry traffic since Year 1?

_____

Plot the data for Tetbury Lane as a bar graph.

Using your graph, decide between which years was the biggest increase in lorry traffic on Tetbury Lane.

_____

This bar chart shows the number of piglets that were born in each litter on Ridgeway Farm during one year.

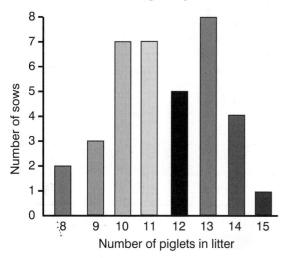

Litter size at Ridgeway Farm

How many sows in total gave birth?

_____

In a good year, the farmer will get over 415 piglets. Was the year illustrated in the bar chart a good year for the farmer?

Yes / No

All the odd numbers between 1 and 20 inclusive were put in a bag and one is pulled out at random. Mark the following on the probability scale below:

A The probability that a number divisible by 5 is pulled out of the bag

B The probability that a prime number is pulled out of the bag

0   0.1   0.2   0.3   0.4   0.5   0.6   0.7   0.8   0.9   1

Which type of graph would best illustrate the rainfall fluctuations over a year?

_____

A market stall sells a range of T-shirts for a number of different prices.

£5.50   £3.99   £7.80   £17.78

£9.99   £15.00   £6.99   £12.95

What is the range of these prices?

_____

What is the mean price of the T-shirts?

_____

Time for a break! Go to Puzzle Page 43 ▶

Total [   ]

Test 13: **Number**

1

Halve 7.58 _____

2

Write in words the number 36 788 001.3

_____

_____

_____

_____

3

Convert 579 g into kg.

_____ kg

4

$9^2 + 12^2 =$ _____

5

Circle an equivalent fraction of $\frac{13}{21}$

A $\frac{26}{45}$

B $\frac{9}{17}$

C $\frac{52}{84}$

D $\frac{38}{42}$

E $\frac{39}{42}$

6

Which two consecutive numbers add up to 57? _____ _____

7

Find the total.

$-39 + -53 =$ _____

8

In a litter of 8 Labrador puppies, 3 were golden and the rest were black. What percentage of the puppies was black? Round your answer to the nearest whole number.

A 8%

B 30%

C 50%

D 63%

E 80%

9

Which number lies midway between 8.96 and 9?

_____

10

Circle the option that correctly completes this problem.

_____ ÷ _____ − _____ = 3.6

A $34 \div 6.2 - 3$

B $36 \div 5 - 3.7$

C $36 \div 6 - 3.4$

D $36 \div 5 - 2.5$

E $36 \div 6 - 2.4$

Total

TEST 14: **Algebra**

1

Complete this sequence.

24 _____ 6 _____ 1.5

2-3

If each row totals 21, what are the values of the letters *a* and *b*?

	a	5	4	2
10	*b*			

a = _____ *b* = _____

4

Write this algebraic expression in its simplest form.

$(6 \times d) + (5 \times d) - d$

_____

5

Find the total if $x = 4$ and $y = 5$

$x + 5y =$ _____

6-7

Write an equation for the following puzzle, then solve it.

Divide *t* by 7, then subtract 6 to get a total of 2.

_____

t = _____

8

Look carefully at the grid below. Write the equation that represents the coordinates plotted. It may help to write out the coordinate pairs.

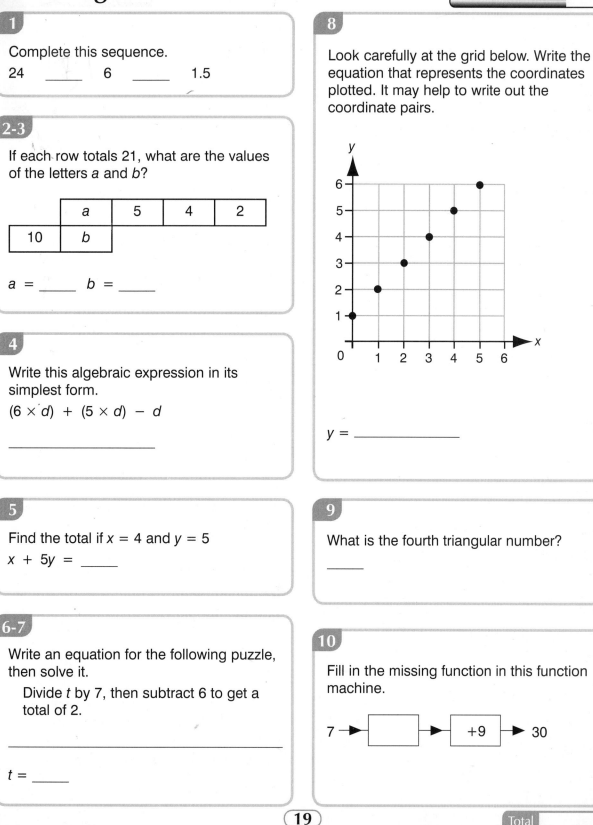

$y =$ _____

9

What is the fourth triangular number?

_____

10

Fill in the missing function in this function machine.

$7 \rightarrow \boxed{} \rightarrow \boxed{+9} \rightarrow 30$

Total

1

Estimate the height and width of a door.

Height = _____

Width = _____

Now find the estimated area of the door.

Area = _____

2

Find the missing angles.

112°

y _____ y

y = _____

3

Mark the parallel // and perpendicular lines ⌐ found in this shape.

4

Name this shape.

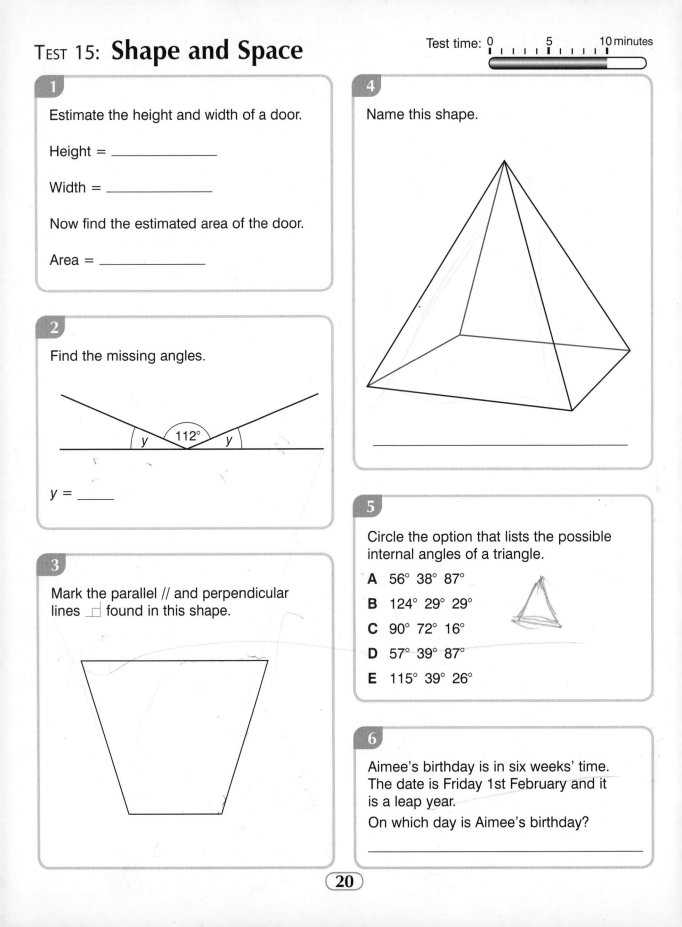

_____

5

Circle the option that lists the possible internal angles of a triangle.

A 56° 38° 87°

B 124° 29° 29°

C 90° 72° 16°

D 57° 39° 87°

E 115° 39° 26°

6

Aimee's birthday is in six weeks' time. The date is Friday 1st February and it is a leap year.

On which day is Aimee's birthday?

_____

Reflect this shape in the line of symmetry.

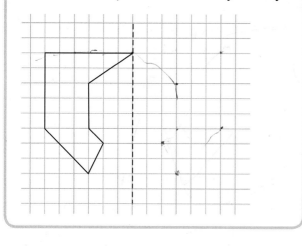

Translate this shape 4 units down and 1 to the left.

You will need to redraw the axes to do this.

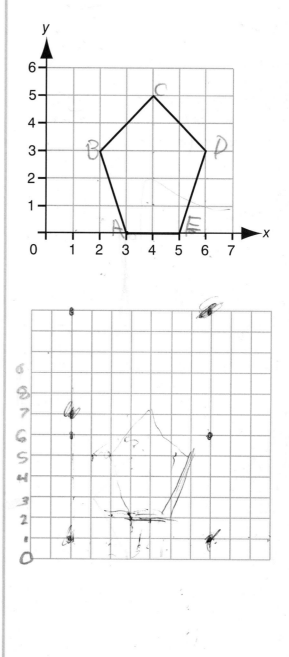

Sketch three rectangles, showing length and width measurements, each with an area of 36 cm².

Total

TEST 16: **Mixed**

1

Change this mixed number to an improper fraction.

$2\frac{3}{8}$ = _____

2

What is 35% of £15.60?
Circle the answer.

A £1.56

B £5

C £5.46

D £7

E £10

3

If the area of a rectangle is 63 cm² and one length is 9 cm, what is the missing length?

9 cm

_____ cm

4

What 3-D shape does this net make?

A tetrahedron

B triangular prism

C square-based pyramid

D octahedron

E icosahedron

5

Find the median of these shoe sizes.

5 6 5 7 4 8 6 8
6 8 7 6 9 7 9 5

Median = _____

6

'Is there a difference between the time boys and girls go to bed?'

Study the question above and state what data would be relevant in investigating it.

_____

_____

_____

7

List all the prime numbers between 20 and 30.

_____

8

Find the input of this function machine.

_____ → × 4 → ÷ 3 → 8

9

A 408 g bar of white chocolate is broken into 12 equal chunks.
How much does one chunk weigh? _____

10

Continue this sequence.

8 13 21 34 _____ _____

Total

TEST 20: Mixed

1-2

Draw an equilateral triangle with each side measuring 3 cm.

What will each inside angle measure?

_____

3

Complete this calculation.

$$\frac{6}{20} = \frac{30}{\underline{\hspace{1cm}}}$$

4

Write the next two triangular numbers.

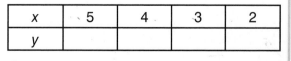

1   3   6   10   _____   _____

5

Make this statement correct by adding < or >.

31.9 ___<___ **32**

6

67% of a 90 g chocolate bar is sugar.
How many grams is this?   _____ g

7-8

Write two questions that would be relevant in a questionnaire looking into television watching patterns of a group of children.

a _____

   _____

b _____

   _____

9-10

Complete this table.
If $y = x - 4$

x	5	4	3	2
y				

Total

1-2

On the axes below, mark the points (4, 2), (4, 0) and (1, 0) and then join them together.

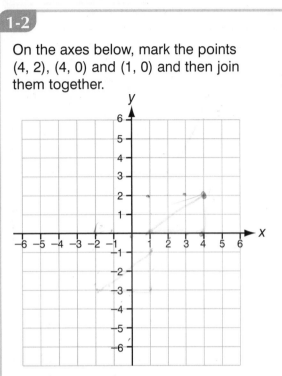

Now translate the shape you have drawn 3 units to the left and 3 units down.

Write the coordinates of the new shape.

(___, ___)

(___, ___)

(___, ___)

3

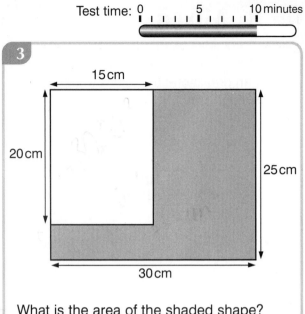

What is the area of the shaded shape?

_____ cm²

4

Complete this function machine with the missing functions.

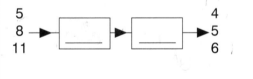

5
8 → [_____] → [_____] → 5
11   6
                          4

5

Sean's mum and dad were buying a new flat screen television.

They found two they liked. Television A was £899 with 5% off. Television B was £1100 with 15% off. They decided to buy the television that cost closest to £900.

Which television did they buy?

_____

Which of these groups of fractions add up to 1?

Circle the answer.

A $\frac{1}{2}$ $\frac{11}{22}$ $\frac{1}{16}$

B $\frac{5}{8}$ $\frac{1}{4}$ $\frac{3}{16}$

C $\frac{1}{5}$ $\frac{3}{15}$ $\frac{6}{10}$

D $\frac{5}{8}$ $\frac{1}{9}$ $\frac{6}{12}$

E $\frac{2}{4}$ $\frac{1}{3}$ $\frac{3}{9}$

Continue this sequence.

123, 109, 95, 81, _____, _____

What is $^-27 + ^-68$? _____

Plot this data on the grid below.

Month	Rainfall (mm)
Jan	56
Feb	62
Mar	77
Apr	45
May	52
Jun	41
Jul	68
Aug	35
Sep	37
Oct	49
Nov	58
Dec	65

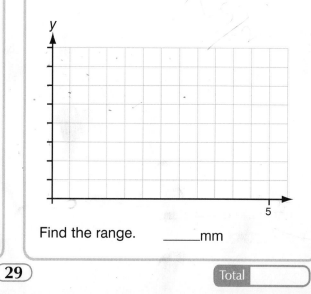

Find the range. _____mm

Total

1-2

Find the mean and median of these shoe sizes.

5 6 8 5 4 6 6 9 5 6 7 7 4 5 6 7

Mean = _____   Median = _____

3

A survey was carried out studying hair colour. The results showed the ratio of blonde children to brown haired children was 2 : 3. If 56 children were blonde, how many were brown haired?

Circle the answer.

A 18   **B** 28   **C** 72   **D** 84   **E** 112

4

What is the missing number?

$4.3 \times \boxed{} = 86$

Circle the answer.

A 2   **B** 20   **C** 21   **D** 200   **E** 23

5

Find the value of x.

$5x - 21 = 14$ $x =$ _____

6

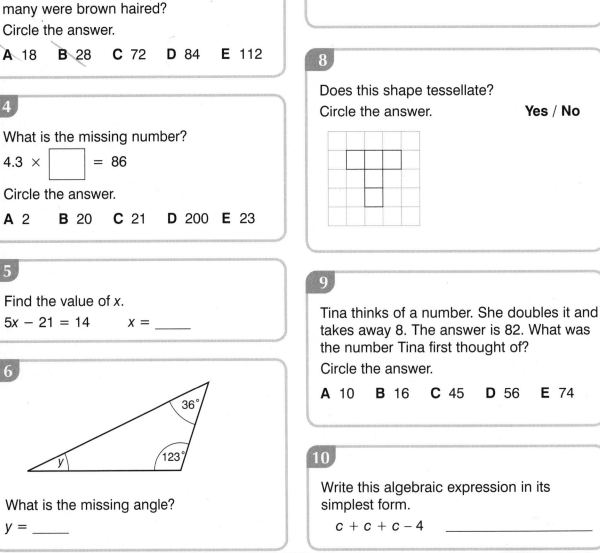

What is the missing angle?

$y =$ _____

7

Draw the net of a cuboid.

8

Does this shape tessellate?

Circle the answer.   **Yes / No**

9

Tina thinks of a number. She doubles it and takes away 8. The answer is 82. What was the number Tina first thought of?

Circle the answer.

A 10   **B** 16   **C** 45   **D** 56   **E** 74

10

Write this algebraic expression in its simplest form.

$c + c + c - 4$ _____

Total

1

Draw a decagon.

2

In a school of 120 children, 45% had school dinners and the rest ate packed lunch. How many children ate packed lunch?

_____

3

Circle the answer to this calculation.

67.9 − 32.68

A 35.32   **B** 34.32   **C** 34.22

D 35.02   **E** 35.22

4

Convert 8% to a fraction in its simplest terms.

_____

5

Which algebraic equation matches the following? Circle the answer.

'*Start with a number. Multiply it by 6 then add 13. The answer is 67.*'

A $6y + 13 = 67$ **B** $y + 13 \times 6 = 67$

C $13 - 6y = 67$ **D** $6 + 13y = 67$

E $y \times 6 - 13 = 67$

6

When a dice is thrown, what is the probability it will land on an even number?

_____

7

Complete the table for a triangular prism.

Faces	
Vertices	
Edges	

8

$15^2 =$ _____

9

Which of these numbers are multiples of 6? Write them on the answer line.

55 72 63 90 36

_____

10

45 m is the same as _____ mm.

Total [ ]

Test time: 0 |||||||||||||| 5 |||||||||||| 10 minutes

1

Find the missing angle.

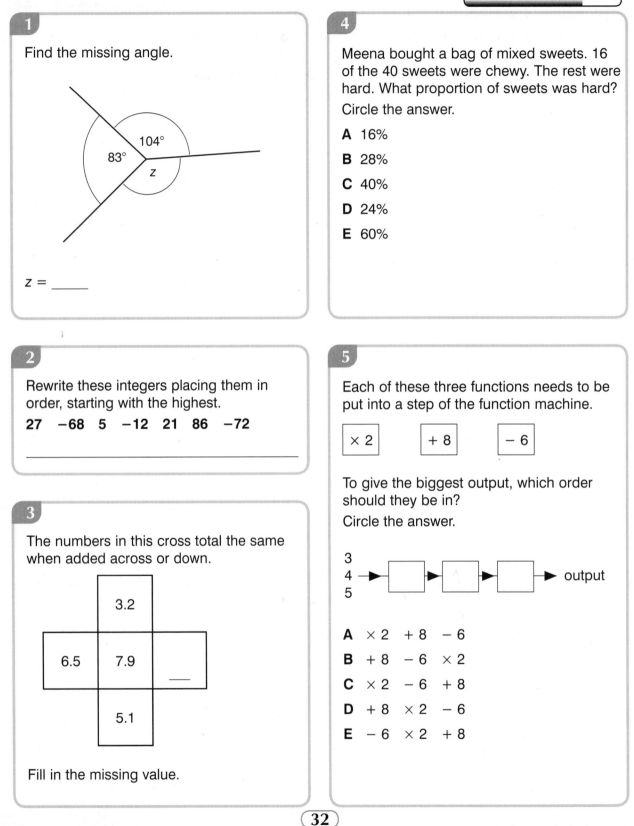

z = _____

2

Rewrite these integers placing them in order, starting with the highest.

27   −68   5   −12   21   86   −72

_____

3

The numbers in this cross total the same when added across or down.

Fill in the missing value.

4

Meena bought a bag of mixed sweets. 16 of the 40 sweets were chewy. The rest were hard. What proportion of sweets was hard?

Circle the answer.

A 16%

B 28%

C 40%

D 24%

E 60%

5

Each of these three functions needs to be put into a step of the function machine.

To give the biggest output, which order should they be in?

Circle the answer.

A × 2   + 8   − 6

B + 8   − 6   × 2

C × 2   − 6   + 8

D + 8   × 2   − 6

E − 6   × 2   + 8

6-7

The data below shows the eye colour of 22 children.

Display this data in an appropriate way on the grid provided below.

grey, blue, grey, blue, brown, brown, blue, grey, blue, brown, grey, blue, brown, brown, blue, grey, brown, blue, blue, blue, brown, grey

8-9

What is the order of rotational symmetry for this square?

_____

How many lines of symmetry does a square have?

_____

10

What is the difference in area between these two rectangles?

15m
2.7m
700cm
900cm

_____ m^2

Time for a break! Go to Puzzle Page 45

Total

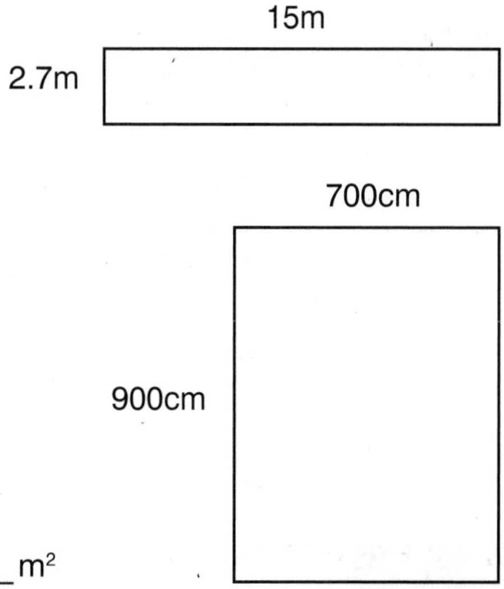

1

What percentage of 6 litres is 3600 ml?
Circle the answer.

A 20%

B 30%

C 49%

D 50%

E 60%

2

Which number lies midway between 5.9
and 6?

_____

3

Reflect this shape in the mirror lines.

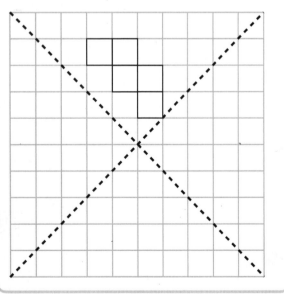

4

What is the value of t in this equation?

$4t - 9 = 23$ $t =$ _____

5

Write the answer to this problem in its
lowest terms.

$4\frac{5}{12} - 2\frac{6}{36} =$ _____

6

Hannah left school at 15:22. She walked
to the bus stop and just caught the bus at
16:01. The bus trip took 18 minutes. She
then walked home from the bus drop off
point, eventually getting in at 16:35.

How long did Hannah spend walking
altogether?

_____

7

How many faces has a dodecahedron?
Circle the answer.

A 5

B 6

C 8

D 10

E 12

8

Round 45 650.5 to the nearest 100.

_____

9-10

Find the mode and mean of these football
fans ages.

| 14 | 34 | 67 | 54 | 34 | 21 | 8 | 9 | 44 |
| 23 | 21 | 19 | 8 | 45 | 66 | 35 | 22 | 34 |

Mode = _____   Mean = _____

Total

Test time: 0 .... 5 .... 10 minutes

1

Simplify this algebraic expression.

$2x + 2x - x$ _____

2

Circle the option that correctly completes this problem.

_____ × _____ + _____ = 40

A $6 \times 6.3 + 5$ **B** $6 \times 4.9 + 10$

C $6 \times 5.1 + 9$ **D** $6.2 \times 6 + 8$

E $6.2 \times 5 + 9$

3-4

Look carefully at these pie charts.

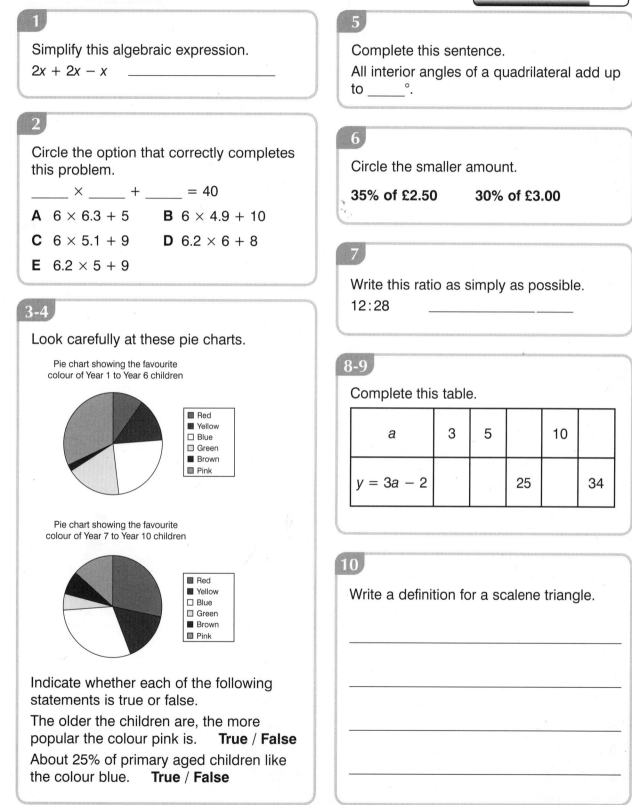

Pie chart showing the favourite colour of Year 1 to Year 6 children

■ Red
■ Yellow
□ Blue
□ Green
■ Brown
□ Pink

Pie chart showing the favourite colour of Year 7 to Year 10 children

■ Red
■ Yellow
□ Blue
□ Green
■ Brown
□ Pink

Indicate whether each of the following statements is true or false.

The older the children are, the more popular the colour pink is.   **True / False**

About 25% of primary aged children like the colour blue.   **True / False**

5

Complete this sentence.

All interior angles of a quadrilateral add up to _____°.

6

Circle the smaller amount.

35% of £2.50   **30% of £3.00**

7

Write this ratio as simply as possible.

12 : 28   _____

8-9

Complete this table.

a	3	5		10	
$y = 3a - 2$			25		34

10

Write a definition for a scalene triangle.

_____

_____

_____

_____

Total

1-2

Represent the following information in the pie chart.

'A survey was conducted at Malmesbury School looking into how the 248 children travelled to school. It was found that 93 walked, 62 rode their bikes, 31 came by bus and the rest travelled by car.'

How many children travelled by car?_____

4

Complete the net of this tetrahedron.

3

How many prime numbers are there between the numbers 6 and 52?

Circle the answer.

A 8

B 10

C 12

D 14

E 16

5

1 kg of beef mince cost £2.48 at Jennings the butchers. How much would 6 kg cost?

Circle the answer.

A £6.48

B £8.50

C £9

D £12.96

E £14.88

6

Complete the missing functions.

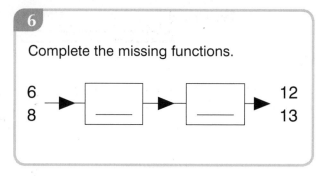

6
8 ▶ ☐ ▶ ☐ ▶ 12
13

7

Draw a quadrilateral with two pairs of equal angles.

8

The perimeter of this shape is 31.8 cm. Find the length of one side.

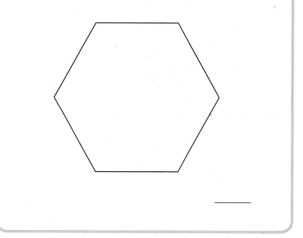

_____

9

When rounded to the nearest whole number, how many of these numbers are rounded up?

4.67   **5.5**   **8.1999**   **3.456**

2.49   **23.9**   **6.919**

_____

10

454 g is the same as 1 lb in weight. Hannah has bought a 5 lb turkey which needs cooking. The instructions state that it needs to be cooked for 55 min per kg + a further 25 min.

Approximately how long does the turkey need to cook for?

Circle the answer.

A $2\frac{1}{2}$ hours

B $1\frac{1}{2}$ hours

C $2\frac{3}{4}$ hours

D 2 hours

E $2\frac{1}{4}$ hours

Total

TEST 28: **Mixed**

1

Circle the prime number.
129   130   131   132   133   134

2

Add the missing sign (<, = or >) in this sentence.
The number of days in November is _____ the number of days in January.

3

What number is the arrow pointing to?

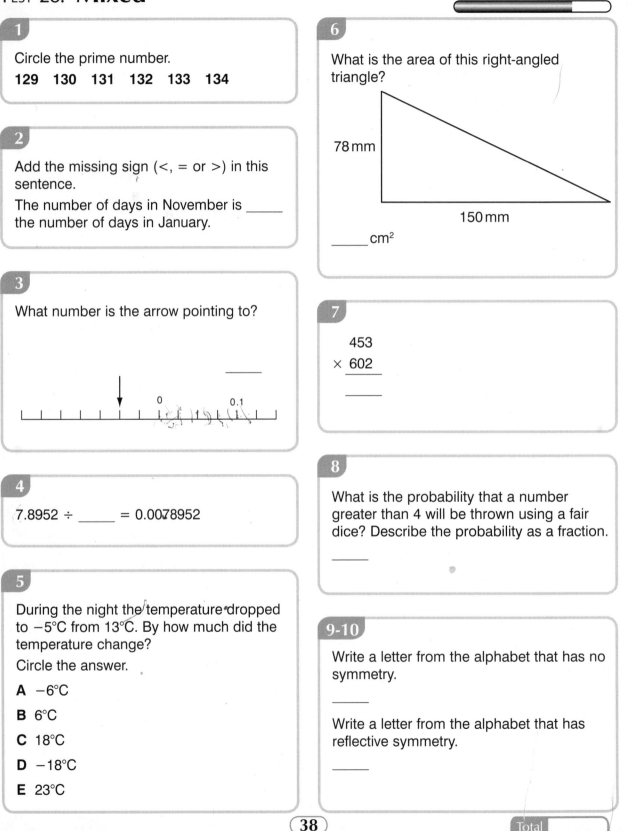

_____

0   0.1

4

7.8952 ÷ _____ = 0.0078952

5

During the night the temperature dropped to −5°C from 13°C. By how much did the temperature change?
Circle the answer.

A −6°C

B 6°C

C 18°C

D −18°C

E 23°C

6

What is the area of this right-angled triangle?

78 mm

150 mm

_____ cm²

7

$$\begin{array}{r} 453 \\ \times\ 602 \\ \hline \\ \hline \end{array}$$

8

What is the probability that a number greater than 4 will be thrown using a fair dice? Describe the probability as a fraction.

_____

9-10

Write a letter from the alphabet that has no symmetry.

_____

Write a letter from the alphabet that has reflective symmetry.

_____

Total [ ]

TEST 29: **Mixed**

1

Write the answer to this problem as an improper fraction in its smallest terms.

$6\frac{5}{18} + 4\frac{5}{6} =$ _____

2

Write this number in words.

123.78

_____

_____

3

Label the two missing internal angles in this triangle.

110°

4-5

Dan made a dice in woodwork. To check his dice wasn't biased he tested it by throwing it 200 times. This table shows his results. Complete the table.

Outcome	1	2	3	4	5	6
Frequency	34	29	47	31	26	

Did Dan discover his dice was biased? Explain your answer.

_____

_____

6

Name two 3-D shapes that can have all their faces identical and regular.

_____   _____

7-8

Find the median and mode of these values.

2.4   3.6   1.8   3.6   3.6   2.4
1.8   2.4   2.2   1.8   3.6

Median = _____   Mode = _____

9

Circle the correct values for x and y if

$7x - y = 12$.

A $x = 5$ $y = 22$

B $x = 4$ $y = 8$

C $x = 5$ $y = 25$

D $x = 3$ $y = 9$

E $x = 4$ $y = 14$

10

Sophie buys a T-shirt for £5.75 and a skirt for £11.99

How much change will she get if she pays with a £20 note?

Circle the answer.

A £2.26

B £6.24

C £8.01

D £14.25

E £17.74

39

Total

1-2

On the grid below, plot the coordinates
(−2, 3), (1, 4), (4, 2), (2, −2) and (−2, −2)
and join them in order.

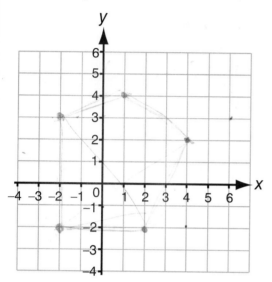

Translate the shape you have drawn 2 to
the right and 1 up.

3

Write down a fraction that is larger than $\frac{15}{21}$
but smaller than $\frac{34}{35}$

_____

4-5

The school dinner ladies at Kingsham
School are concerned about the amount
of food that is wasted each mealtime. They
decide to do a survey to try to find the
cause.

Who might they aim the survey at?

_____

_____

List three questions that they should
include in their survey.

a _____

_____

_____

b _____

_____

_____

c _____

_____

_____

6

25 mm is the same as _____ cm.

7

Draw a nonagon.

9

These ingredients are needed to make 60 Butter Biscuits.

175 g soft unsalted butter

200 g caster sugar

3 large eggs

1 teaspoon vanilla

400 g plain flour

300 g icing sugar

Write out the ingredients again so the recipe will make 20 Butter Biscuits.

____

____

____

____

____

____

8

Write down the first four numbers in this sequence using the information below.

'The second number is 9. Each number is a third of the previous number'

_____ _____ _____ _____

10

Write the following in the form of an algebraic expression.

6 times *d* add half of *e*

____

Total

Time for a break! Go to Puzzle Page 46

Puzzle ❶

Look carefully at the triangles below. There is a hidden pattern in the numbers found in each triangle.

Can you solve the pattern and complete the final triangle?

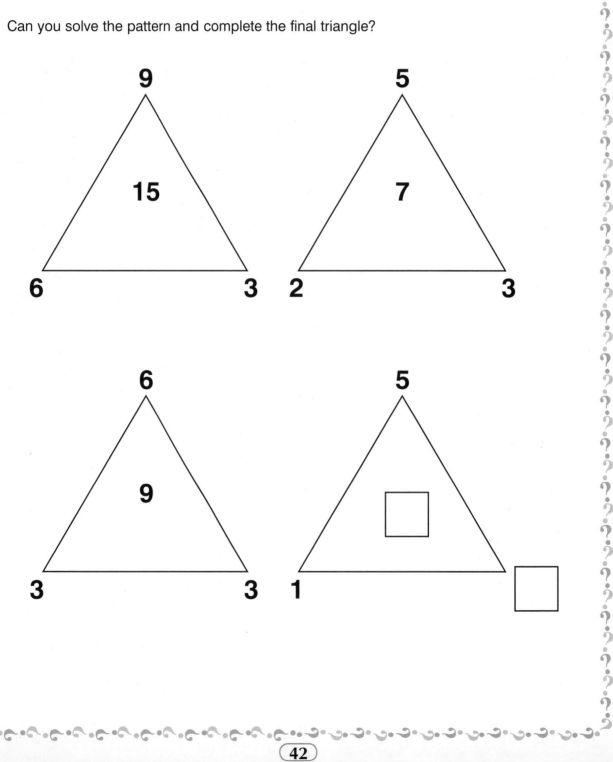

Puzzle ❷

Circle all the capital letters in the alphabet that have an order of rotational symmetry of two.

A	B	C	D	E	F
G	H	I	J	K	L
M	N	O	P	Q	R
S	T	U	V	W	X
		Y	Z		

Underline the letters which have reflective symmetry.

Which of the letters above have both reflective and rotational symmetry?

_____

Puzzle ❸

Joe's Jeans is having an end of season sale.
A number of jeans have a percentage off the full price.

What was the original price of each pair of jeans?

20% OFF

NOW £23.99

75% OFF

NOW £30.00

55% OFF

NOW £22.28

Original price: _____   **Original price:** _____   **Original price:** _____

A week later the prices of all three pairs of jeans were cut by a further 50% off the sale price. If you bought all three pairs now, how much change would you have from £100.00?

_____

What overall saving would you make from the original price of the jeans?

_____

Puzzle 4

How close can you get?

Using only the numbers on the cards and whichever operations you need
(+, −, × and ÷), try to get as close as you can to the number in the star.
You must use all the numbers, but only once each.
You can use each operation as many times as you like.

| 67 | 9 | 2 | 12 | 6 |

★ 456

Write your closest calculation here:

___444_____

Try this again but this time ask someone else to provide
a new total to aim for!

Puzzle ⑤

A farmer grows 195 kg of potatoes.
To sell them on, he needs to divide them into 5 kg and 2.5 kg bags.
He needs an equal number of each size bag.

A. How many bags of each weight does 195 kg make?

_____ 2.5 kg bags

_____ 5 kg bags

B. The farmer now needs to put the bags into boxes. Each box can hold
20 kg of weight. How many boxes does the farmer need?

_____

Use the space here to work out your answer.

Progress Grid

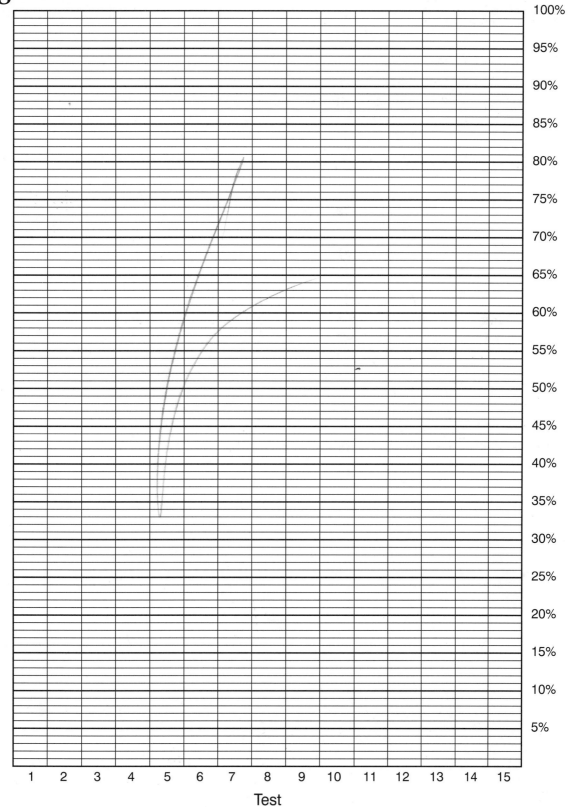

Total marks

Test

Progress Grid

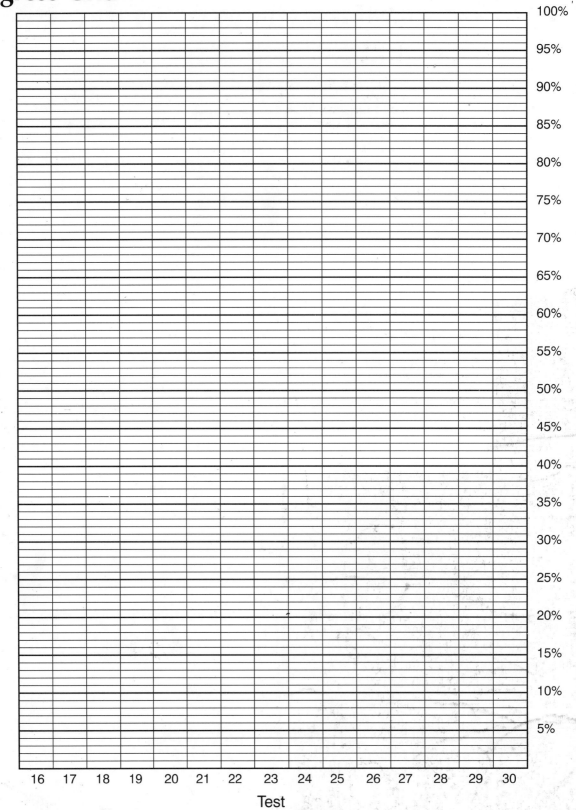

Total marks

100%
95%
90%
85%
80%
75%
70%
65%
60%
55%
50%
45%
40%
35%
30%
25%
20%
15%
10%
5%

16 17 18 19 20 21 22 23 24 25 26 27 28 29 30

Test